How to Use This Book

★ Meeting the NCTM Standards ★

The National Council of Teachers of Mathematics (NCTM) has proposed standards that emphasize the importance of including problem solving, logical reasoning, and communication in every mathematics program, beginning with the very youngest student. *First Word Problems: Time & Money* assists you the teacher in developing children's logical reasoning and numeration skills. Through these problem-solving experiences, students learn to analyze numbers, to develop logical thinking skills, and to communicate about mathematics. *First Word Problems: Time & Money* is a stimulating way to include all children in a mathematical discussion and to encourage students to think about how numbers relate to one another and to the world around them. Additionally, it provides authentic reading and writing experiences for young children as they read the clues to solve the word problems and write their own word problem clues for others to solve. Children will discover that meeting the NCTM standards has never been more engaging or more fun.

★ Getting Started ★

Gathering Materials

To make teaching time and money math concepts easier and more manageable, we've provided reproducible, riddle-style word problems that build problem-solving skills. First, students read the word problems and identify key information. Then, they use reproducible clocks and coins to explore the concepts presented in the word problems and show what they know. The manipulatives are easy to assemble, so each student can make a set to work with and problem solve. The manipulatives are portable as well, so children can work on their math problems at their desks, in centers, or at home.

The reproducible templates include

- an analog clock with movable hands for modeling and practicing telling time (page 60),
- a set of coins that include both "heads" and "tails" for counting money (page 61),
- a pocket for storing coins and hiding correct answers (page 63),
- blank templates students can use to write original word problems (page 64).

Adding Your Own Materials

You may find it helpful to supplement the reproducibles in this book with additional educational materials and tools.

Chart Paper Print word problems on large sheets of chart paper, writing the different lines in alternating colors (blue clue, red clue, blue clue, red clue) to help children discriminate between clues. That way, as the class solves the problems together, each child can easily read the clues. Additionally, you can use the chart as a source for word study or word wall words.

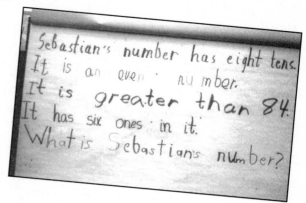

Overhead Projector Use a photocopier to make word problem transparencies. Display the word problems on an overhead projector so children can read the clues along with you as you solve the word problems together.

Highlighting Tape Make use of highlighting tape to draw attention to frequently used words such as *what, is, my, the,* and so on. Highlighting tape is available at most teacher supply stores.

Analog Clocks Ask children to set analog clocks to the times shown on the time word problems. Store the clocks in a math center for students to use as needed.

Plastic Coins Provide plastic coins for children to use as they solve money word problems. Store the coins in a piggy bank in your math center. Or, invite students to make a pocket in which to store their own sets of coins. A pocket template has been provided for this purpose. (See page 63.)

Magnetic Coins Consider creating magnetic coins by placing magnetic tape on the back of real, paper (page 61), or plastic coins. Then have children work on solving their money word problems on metal surfaces, such as cookie trays.

Making the Most of the Word Problems

In this resource, you'll find sixty word problems, thirty for time and thirty for money. All of the word problems are numbered to help make record keeping easier. As the numbers go up, the problems increase in difficulty.

For suggested steps and recommendations about instruction, read Introducing Word Problems to Students on page 11. Then, select the word problems on which you'll focus and begin your math lesson.

Time

The word problems for time begin on page 19. They integrate logic with telling time on analog clocks. Write-on lines are provided under the analog clock representations with each word problem to record the digital time before solving the problems. The answer key is on page 58.

Money

The word problems for money begin on page 40. They focus on problem solving with coin values and coin recognition. You may wish to keep the "change" in a pocket to be revealed when the riddle is solved. After becoming accustomed to the style and format of the money word problems, students may enjoy taking turns manipulating the money and keeping the change in a pocket. It can be a pocket in clothing or a paper pocket made with the template provided on page 63. The answer key is on page 59.

If you're working on a word problem as a whole group, it is helpful to generate a list of possible answers with children. It is also helpful to have the correct answer available in a visual form (written on a card, in coins, or on an analog clock). Having the answer represented in this way allows students to concretely confirm their answers, and provides a sense of closure to the problem.

Assembling the Manipulatives

Making the Clock

Use this analog clock model to help students learn about measuring time.

Materials

◆ copies of reproducible page 60

◆ scissors

◆ colored pencils, crayons, or markers (optional)

Guide children in following these directions:

1. Color the clock parts, if desired.

2. Cut out the clock and hands.

3. Place the short arrow on top of the long arrow, so the rounded end and the arrow points match up.

4. Center the rounded ends on top of the black dot of the clock face. Hold the arrows in place.

5. Push the brass fastener tabs through the rounded-end of the arrows and the clock face. Fold the fastener tabs back to secure all the pieces in place.

Making the Coins

Use these coins to help students learn about counting money.

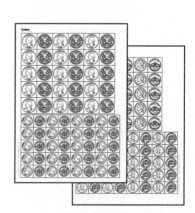

Materials

◆ copies of reproducible pages 61 and 62

◆ scissors

◆ colored pencils, crayons, or markers (optional)

Guide children in following these directions:

1. Color the coins, if desired.

2. Cut out the coin patterns.

3. Fold the patterns along the solid line, so corners

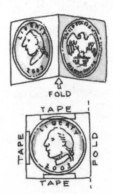

match up and the coins' "heads" sides and "tails" sides face outward.

4. Tape each coin pattern together, applying tape along the open sides.

Making the Pocket

Use this pocket to store coins and hide answers.

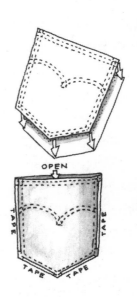

Materials

- two copies of reproducible page 63
- scissors
- tape
- colored pencils, crayons, or markers (optional)
- brass fastener

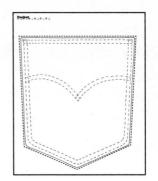

Guide children in following these directions:

1. Color the pockets, if desired.

2. Cut out the pockets.

3. Place the pockets on top of each other, so the corners match up and the colored sides face outward.

4. Tape the pockets together by applying tape on four sides, leaving the top of the pocket open and functional.

★ Integrating Word Problems Into the Curriculum ★

Because literacy experts recommend at least a two-hour literacy block in students' daily schedules, integrating instruction is one way to maximize limited instructional time. *First Word Problems: Time & Money* provides a way to integrate curriculum. Through the use of language-rich word problems children are involved in purposeful reading and writing experiences, while exercising their logical reasoning skills. In addition, students practice key reading and writing skills as they gather information, communicate, and demonstrate knowledge.

There are several ways to fit word problems into a demanding curriculum. Some suggestions follow:

During the Math Block

◆ Present a word problem at the beginning of the math lesson as a warm-up or at the end of the math lesson as a wrap-up.

◆ Use a word problem to introduce a new mathematical concept. (In other words, the word problem can BE your math lesson.)

◆ Post the word problem in a classroom center as a challenge of the day or a problem of the week; have students work on it in pairs or individually; discuss it as a whole group when the allotted time has ended.

◆ While children are working in centers, give them the option of writing original word problems either independently or in pairs. (The reproducibles on page 64 can be used for this purpose.)

◆ Have one or two students share their original word problems at the end of math time. You may want to work with the child ahead of time to refine the clues. Alternatively, present the sharing time as a time for the class to help the student refine his or her clues—a strategy similar to the author's chair during writing workshop. The child can read the clues to the class; if more clues are needed to solve the word problem, the class can ask questions to help the student add more clues.

During the Literacy Block

◆ Read word problems during shared reading to "double up" on math and reading time. The word problems provide another style of text to engage children in shared reading. The repetitive language of the clues, the familiar mathematical terms, and the predictable structure of the word problems make them ideal for shared reading and add variety to your repertoire of materials. Reread previously solved word problems to engage reluctant readers and to increase students' word recognition and reading fluency.

◆ Reread previously solved word problems as a basis for word study. The word problems can be used to identify and highlight frequently used words. You can also create a math word wall to post familiar mathematical terms (i.e. *hour, minute, coin, clock*). Children can refer to these words when they are writing their own

word problems or in their journal-writing about other mathematical concepts.

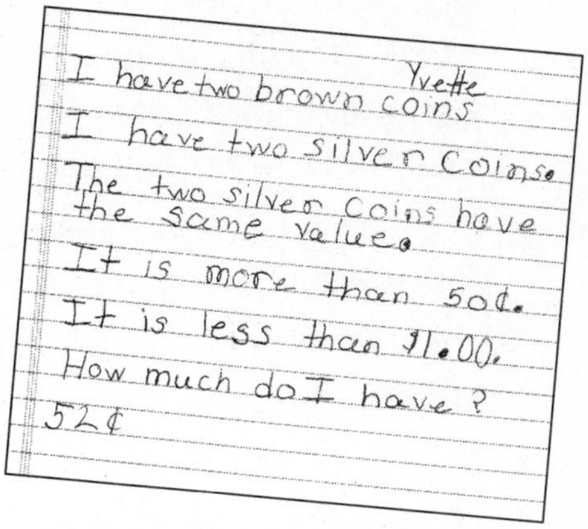

◆ Include a word problem at a center to provide experience reading for a specific purpose (to solve the word problem) and across the content areas.

◆ Provide children with opportunities at the writing center to write word problems.

◆ Post the students' original word problems for children to read when "reading around the room." (Classroom volunteers can help with the task of typing student word problems.)

[handwritten note]
I have two brown coins   Yvette
I have two silver coins.
The two silver coins have
the same value.
It is more than 50¢.
It is less than $1.00.
How much do I have?
52¢

◆ Allow students to read their original word problems to each other and to class volunteers in order to encourage rereadings and good listening.

◆ Use children's first drafts of original word problems to engage them in revising their work for others to read. Students can use a colored pencil to add punctuation and capital letters and to check spelling. This can be done during an individual writing conference if the child is ready to work on revision. Otherwise, students can read their word problems to classroom volunteers as they type, if there is a need for the word problems to be in standard spelling.

◆ As a class, children can create their own word problems. (See Writing Word Problems on page 16 and the Write Your Own Word Problem reproducible templates on page 64.)

★ Introducing Word Problems to Students ★

Children feel most successful with word problems if the problems are introduced slowly. Students should not be expected to solve the word problems alone; rather, these problems are a wonderful tool to use in helping children clarify their understanding of mathematical ideas through discussion and writing.

The following are tried and true directions for using word problems with children:

1. Put a word problem on an overhead projector or chart, or use it in its original format with a small group of students. If rewriting the clues, use two different colored markers to alternate the colors of the clues on the chart in order to help

children discriminate between clues. Provide manipulatives for students to use while solving the word problems. (Children may need practice in using these manipulatives at first.) Use an empty chart to record the children's thinking.

2. If working with the time word problems, begin by having children identify the times represented on the analog clocks at the top of the page. Record the time on the write-on line beneath each analog clock.

3. Begin with all but the first clue covered. Have the class read the first clue together. Then based on that clue, have children discuss all the possible solutions. This first clue is usually very broad, providing opportunities for shy or less verbal children to participate in the discussion, since there is typically a wide range of answers at this point.

4. Uncover the second clue and read it together. Ask students to eliminate—based on this new information—answers they previously thought possible. As children recommend that a solution be eliminated, have them explain why it is no longer a possibility. (As students become more familiar with word problems, this is also a wonderful opportunity to have children write their explanations.) Some of the best "teachable moments" spring up in these discussions, which often present opportunities to introduce, clarify, or recall mathematical concepts. Because of all the problem-solving and mathematical concepts imbedded in each of these word problems, this alone may constitute the entire math lesson—especially when the word problems are first introduced. Through these discussions and in their writing, students are refining their thinking and expressing themselves mathematically.

5. Uncover the third clue and read it together. Continue to eliminate the possibilities for the unknown solution. Continue in this fashion until the solution is determined. As you discuss the possibilities for the word problem, direct children to reread the clues that have been uncovered to remind them of the information they have already gathered.

As an alternative to following these steps, reveal all the clues of a particular word problem at once, then have the students use the clues in their own way to figure out the solution by working in pairs or small groups. Engage children in a class discussion to enable them to share their thinking and to discuss the mathematical concepts involved in that particular problem.

Sample Lesson
◆·◆·◆·◆·◆·◆·◆·◆· ⑨

(Teacher-Student Dialogue for Money Word Problem #6, page 42)
This word problem focuses primarily on the value of the coins. It is a whole-class
lesson with the math problem on an overhead projector or on chart paper with large
enough print for the whole class to view. Prior to the lesson, the teacher has placed a
nickel in her pocket.

Teacher: "Let's read the first clue together: I have one coin in my pocket.
What do you think that coin could be

Students: "Penny! Dime!"

Teacher: [Teacher records as children list the possibilities.]
"Could I have any other coins in my pocket?"

Students: "Nickel! Quarter!"
[Teacher continues to record responses.]

Teacher: "Okay, let's read the next clue together. I have more than 3¢.
Could I still have a penny in my pocket?"
[Teacher refers to student responses.]

Students: "No, it's only 1¢." If children say: "Yes," the teacher could then ask,
"What is the value of the penny?" to help the students realize it coul
not be a penn
[Teacher crosses "penny" off the possibility list.]

Teacher: "Could I still have a dime in my pocket?"

Students: "Yes."

Teacher: "Why do you think so?"

Students: "Because a dime is 10¢."

Teacher: "Is 10¢ more than 3¢?"

Students: "Yes."

Teacher: "Then it could still be a dime. Could it still be a nickel?"

Students: "Yes, because it is 5¢."

Teacher: "Is 5¢ more than 3¢?

Students: "Yes."

Teacher: "Then I could have a nickel in my pocket. Could I still have a quarter?"
[Teacher continues in this fashion through all of the possibilities to model thinking through the problem.]

Teacher: "Okay, let's read the last clue together: I have less than 10¢.
What do you think? Could I still have a dime in my pocket?

Students: "Yes! It's 10¢!"

Teacher: "The clue says my coin is *less than* 10¢. Less than doesn't include 10¢.
It is all of the values *before* 10¢. What are those values?

Students: 9¢, 5¢, 3¢
[Teacher records values as children list them.]

Teacher: Anything else? Let's look at our hundred chart to see if we have all of the values before 10.

Students: 8¢, 7¢, 6¢, 4¢, 2¢, 1¢

Teacher: So could I still have a dime in my pocket if the coin is *less than* 10¢?

Students: "No, it can't be a dime."
[Teacher crosses it off the possibility list.]

Teacher: "Could it still be a nickel?"

Students: "Yes! It's less than 10¢!"

Teacher: "Is it more than 3¢, like this clue says my coin is?"
[Teacher refers back to the riddle's second clue.]

Students: "Yes!"

Teacher: "Okay, so it could be a nickel in my pocket. Could it still be a quarter?"

Students: "No, a quarter is 25¢. That's *more than* 10¢."

Teacher: "Okay, so it can't be a quarter. Let's look at what we have left."

Students: "You have a nickel in your pocket!"

Teacher: "Let's check the clues. Is it one coin?"
[Teacher refers to written clues.]

Students: "Yes!"

Teacher: "Is the value more than 3¢?"

Students: "Yes!"

Teacher: "Is the value less than 10¢?"

Students: "Yes!"

Teacher: "Then it must be a nickel. Let's see!"
[Teacher removes nickel from his/her pocket to show children.]
"Is this a nickel?"

Students: "It's a nickel!"

Differentiating Instruction

After students have had sufficient time to explore word problems, place the word problems at a center. Children can work with a partner or in a small group to support each other. If a particular group of students needs a challenge, have them work on a more complex word problem together while you work with the rest of the class on another.

The task of creating original word problems is also a way to challenge students who are ready for more complex problem-solving experiences. Children can use their developmental spelling for the first draft, and teachers or classroom volunteers can type the drafts with standard spelling for posting on the wall for others to read. Student collaboration is again a supportive way for children to create a word problem. In fact, we have seen several reluctant writers find new inspiration when writing word problems, particularly when the option of working with a peer is made available.

The manipulatives make solving the word problems possible for a variety of learners. Call on children needing more support in the beginning of the discussion, after the first or second clue is revealed, when the range of responses is greater. This will help to increase student confidence and facilitate learning. Children who require a challenge can be asked to refine the answer when the choices are fewer. The format of the word problems allows for all learners to participate.

★ Writing Word Problems ★

Writing word problems is another way to assess children's understanding of the concepts taught. It allows you to note what concepts need to be further studied or reinforced.

Writing as a Class

With enough practice solving them, students can create their own word problems together as a class. Frequently, children will begin informally offering a single clue about a number they have in their head to a classmate or to the teacher. They may also report their efforts to share a word problem

at home. These little signs indicate a good time to begin an original class word problem. If you are hesitant to have your class write a word problem from scratch, you could begin one and have children help you finish it.

To begin writing, follow these steps:

1. Follow the format of the style of word problem with which you have been working (for example, money). With students, look back at other word problem charts you have already used and notice some of the patterns of the clues (value of coins, number of coins, or color of coins, for example).

2. Provide coins for the children to manipulate as they create the word problem. Ask one student to select some coins near you and the easel. Guide the rest of the children in asking questions about the student's coins. *(Do you have one coin? Is the value of your coin greater than 20¢?)*

3. After each question, help children decide on the clue *(I have more than one coin)* before writing.

4. Continue this until the students have solved the word problem and written the clues on the easel. To maintain child interest, it may be necessary to take more than one writing session to complete the word problem. In this case, recording the student's coins and keeping it somewhere "safe" usually works well.

As an alternative, have the class decide together on an amount, rather than asking just one child to do this. Set a purpose for the creation of the word problem (for another familiar adult in the building to solve, for example). Then, write the clues together, as described in the steps above.

Writing Independently

Students can write about the strategies they use to solve word problems. As they write about which clues were helpful and why, children further develop their logical reasoning skills. In addition, it provides students with additional purposeful writing experiences. This is a wonderful entry for the math journal, where children can keep a record of their progress in expressing themselves mathematically through writing. These entries serve as informal writing assessments with which teachers may note growth in spelling, the use of capital letters and punctuation, and writing fluency over time.

To facilitate the independent writing of original word problems, engage students in several class writing experiences first. Subsequently, provide children with the choice of writing word problems, among other writing choices, in the writing or math centers. Post a previously-solved problem as an example or make a photocopy of one of the Write Your Own Word Problem templates on page 64 for each child, and have students try writing word problems. Many children are more successful working as part of a pair at first. After all of this experience, children will be prepared to successfully work at a more independent level.

Tip!

If you plan to use the writing templates, you might consider using a photocopier to increase their size. First, make a photocopy of page 64. Then, cut the page in half and use the enlargement feature to make photocopies of both templates. Students will appreciate having plenty of room to write.

___ : ___   ___ : ___   ___ : ___

The hands on my clock are in a straight line.

Both hands on my clock point to the same number.

What time does my clock show?

___ : ___   ___ : ___   ___ : ___

The hands on my clock do **not** show 12:00.

The hands on my clock do **not** show 10:00.

What time does my clock show?

___ : ___   ___ : ___   ___ : ___

My clock does **not** show 12:00.

The hands on my clock show that the hour hand is on the 4.

What time does my clock show?

___ : ___   ___ : ___   ___ : ___

My clock does **not** show 8:00.

My clock does **not** show noon.

What time does my clock show?

___ : ___   ___ : ___   ___ : ___

The hands on my clock are **not** close together.

The hands on my clock show that the time is earlier than 5:00.

What time does my clock show?

___ : ___   ___ : ___   ___ : ___

The hands on my clock show that the time is exactly on the hour.

The hands on my clock show that the time is midnight.

What time does my clock show?

____ : ____   ____ : ____   ____ : ____

The minute hand on my clock points to the 12.

The hour hand on my clock shows a time before 3:00.

The hour hand on my clock shows a time after 1:00.

What time does my clock show?

_____ : _____   _____ : _____   _____ : _____

The hands on my clock show that the time is later than 2:00.

The hands on my clock show that the time is earlier than 3:00.

What time does my clock show?

_____ : _____   _____ : _____   _____ : _____

The minute hand on my clock shows 30 minutes after the hour.

The hour hand on my clock points to the 3.

What time does my clock show?

_____:_____   _____:_____   _____:_____   _____:_____

The hands on my clock show that the time is exactly on the hour.

The hands on my clock are in a straight line.

The hands on my clock show that the time is later than 4:00.

What time does my clock show?

___ : ___   ___ : ___   ___ : ___

The hands on my clock show that the time is later than 9:00.

The hands on my clock show that the time is **not** half past the hour.

What time does my clock show?

___ : ___   ___ : ___   ___ : ___

The hands on my clock show that the time is **not** 4:00.

The minute hand on my clock is pointing to the 6.

What time does my clock show?

___ : ___   ___ : ___   ___ : ___   ___ : ___

The hands on my clock show that the time is earlier than 4:00.

The hands on my clock show that the time is later than 12:30.

The hands on my clock show that it is half past the hour.

What time does my clock show?

___ : ___   ___ : ___   ___ : ___   ___ : ___

The hands on my clock show that the time is half past the hour.

The hands on my clock show that the time is earlier than 3:00.

The hands on my clock show that it is closer to 12:00 than to 2:00.

What time does my clock show?

___ : ___   ___ : ___   ___ : ___   ___ : ___

The hands on my clock show that the time
is earlier than 8:00.

The minute hand on my clock points to the 12.

The hands on my clock show that
it is later than 6:00.

What time does my clock show?

___ : ___   ___ : ___   ___ : ___   ___ : ___   ___ : ___

The hands on my clock show that the time is half past the hour.

The hands on my clock show that the time is later than 12:00.

The hands on my clock show that it is earlier than 3:00.

What time does my clock show?

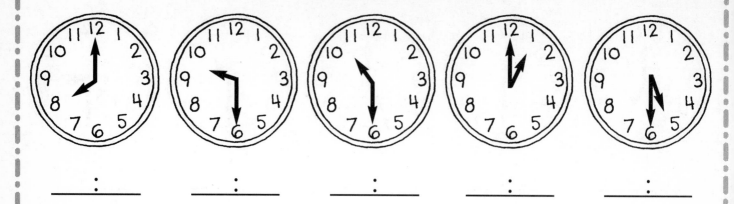

____ : ____   ____ : ____   ____ : ____   ____ : ____   ____ : ____

The hands on my clock show that the time is half past the hour.

The hands on my clock show that the time is before 12:00.

The hands on my clock show that it is after 10:00.

What time does my clock show?

___ : ___   ___ : ___   ___ : ___   ___ : ___

The hour hand on my clock points to 2.

The minute hand on my clock shows that the time is 15 minutes after the hour.

What time does my clock show?

___ : ___   ___ : ___   ___ : ___

The hands on my clock show that the time is later than 9:00.

The hands on my clock show that the time is later than 9:45.

What time does my clock show?

___ : ___   ___ : ___   ___ : ___

The hands on my clock show that the time is half past the hour.

The hands on my clock show that the time is later than 2:00.

What time does my clock show?

___ : ___   ___ : ___   ___ : ___

The hands on my clock show that the time is later than 4:00.

The hands on my clock show that the time is earlier than 4:30.

What time does my clock show?

___ : ___   ___ : ___   ___ : ___   ___ : ___

The hands on my clock show that it is 15 minutes past the hour.

The hands on my clock show that the time is later than 5:30.

The hands on my clock show that it is earlier than 7:00.

What time does my clock show?

___ : ___   ___ : ___   ___ : ___   ___ : ___

The hands on my clock show that the time is past noon.

The hands on my clock show that the time is earlier than 6:30.

The hands on my clock show that it is 15 minutes after the hour.

What time does my clock show?

___ : ___   ___ : ___   ___ : ___   ___ : ___

The hands on my clock show that the time is 45 minutes past the hour.

The hands on my clock show that the time is 15 minutes before 10:00.

What time does my clock show?

___ : ___   ___ : ___   ___ : ___   ___ : ___

The hands on my clock show that the time is after 5:00.

The hands on my clock show that the time is earlier than 6:30.

What time does my clock show?

___ : ___   ___ : ___   ___ : ___   ___ : ___

The hands on my clock show that the time
is half past the hour.

The hands on my clock show that the time
is later than 7:00.

The hands on my clock show that
it is earlier than 8:00.

What time does my clock show?

___ : ___   ___ : ___   ___ : ___   ___ : ___

The hands on my clock show that the time is 15 minutes past the hour.

The hands on my clock show that it is earlier than 7:00.

The hands on my clock show that it is later than 1:00.

What time does my clock show?

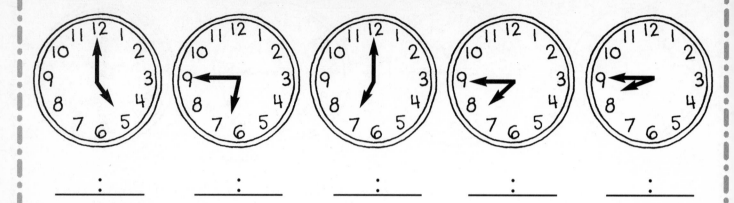

___ : ___   ___ : ___   ___ : ___   ___ : ___   ___ : ___

The hands on my clock show that it is 45 minutes after the hour.

The hands on my clock show that the time is later than 7:00.

The hands on my clock show that it is 15 minutes before 9:00.

What time does my clock show?

____ : ____   ____ : ____   ____ : ____

The hands on my clock show a time
when we are at school.

The hands on my clock show that it is later than 12:00.

What time does my clock show?

____ : ____   ____ : ____   ____ : ____

The hands on my clock show that the time
is later than 5:00.

The minute hand on my clock is pointing to the 5.

What time does my clock show?

I have one coin in my pocket.

The value of my coin is less than 4¢.

What is the change in my pocket?

I have two coins in my pocket.

The value of my coins is 2¢.

Both coins are brown.

What is the change in my pocket?

I have one coin in my pocket.

My coin is silver.

The value of my coin is 10¢.

What is the change in my pocket?

I have three coins in my pocket.

I have less than 10¢.

I have less than 5¢.

What is the change in my pocket?

I have one coin in my pocket.

My coin is less than a dime.

My coin is silver.

What is the change in my pocket?

I have one coin in my pocket.

I have more than 3¢.

I have less than 10¢.

What is the change in my pocket?

I have one coin in my pocket.

My coin is a silver coin.

My coin is larger than a dime.

My coin is less than 10¢.

What is the change in my pocket?

I have two identical coins in my pocket.

My coins total less than 20¢.

My coins are both brown.

What is the change in my pocket?

I have three identical coins in my pocket.

My coins total less than 20¢.

My coins are all silver.

What is the change in my pocket?

I have one coin in my pocket.

My coin is worth more than 1¢.

My coin is worth more than 5¢.

My coin is worth less than 25¢.

What is the change in my pocket?

First Word Problems: Time & Money Scholastic Teaching Resources, page 45

I have four identical coins in my pocket.

I have less than 40¢.

I have less than 20¢.

What is the change in my pocket?

I have four identical coins in my pocket.

I have less than 50¢.

I have more than 30¢.

What is the change in my pocket?

I have less than 10¢ in my pocket.

I have one coin.

I have more than 1¢.

What is the change in my pocket?

I have two identical coins in my pocket.

I have more than 10¢.

I have less than 50¢.

What is the change in my pocket?

I have one coin in my pocket.

My coin is less than 25¢.

My coin and a nickel equal 6¢.

What is the change in my pocket?

I have one coin in my pocket.

The value of my coin is more than 5¢.

My coin and a dime equal 35¢.

What is the change in my pocket?

I have two identical coins in my pocket.

The change in my pocket is less than 20¢.

I have more than 3¢ in my pocket.

What is the change in my pocket?

I have two coins in my pocket.

Both coins are silver.

The value of my coins is 20¢.

What is the change in my pocket?

I have three different coins in my pocket.

I have two silver coins and one brown coin.

The value of each of my coins is less than 25¢.

What is the change in my pocket?

I have less than 25¢ in my pocket.

I have four coins.

My coins are silver.

What is the change in my pocket?

I have two coins in my pocket.

I have a large coin and a small coin.

I have more than 25¢.

I have less than 30¢.

What is the change in my pocket?

I have two coins in my pocket.

The coins in my pocket are the same.

The coins equal more than 20¢.

The coins do **not** equal $1.00.

What is the change in my pocket?

I have two coins in my pocket.

I do **not** have quarters.

My coins are **not** identical.

I have less than 10¢.

What is the change in my pocket?

I have three coins in my pocket.

I do **not** have quarters.

Two of my coins are identical.

I have less than 10¢.

What is the change in my pocket?

I have three coins that are all different.

One of my coins is a penny.

Two of my coins are silver.

I do **not** have a dime.

I have less than 35¢.

What is the change in my pocket?

I have less than 50¢ in my pocket.

I have more than 30¢.

I have five coins.

I have only two dimes.

I do **not** have pennies.

What is the change in my pocket?

I have less than 60¢ in my pocket.

I have more than 25¢.

I have two coins.

Both coins are identical.

What is the change in my pocket?

I have less than 20¢ in my pocket.

The change in my pocket is an even number.

I have five coins.

One of my coins is a dime.

I have three different types of coins.

What is the change in my pocket?

I have less than 15¢ in my pocket.

The change in my pocket is an odd number.

I have three coins.

One of my coins is a nickel.

What is the change in my pocket?

I have three coins in my pocket.

I have more than 50¢.

I have less than 60¢.

One of my coins is a nickel.

What is the change in my pocket?

Answer Key

TIME

Problem	Answer		Problem	Answer
#1	12:00		#16	1:30
#2	11:00		#17	10:30
#3	4:00		#18	2:15
#4	9:00		#19	10:00
#5	4:00		#20	2:30
#6	12:00		#21	4:15
#7	2:00		#22	6:15
#8	2:30		#23	6:15
#9	3:30		#24	9:45
#10	6:00		#25	6:15
#11	10:00		#26	7:30
#12	11:30		#27	1:15
#13	3:30		#28	8:45
#14	12:30		#29	12:25
#15	7:00		#30	6:25

Answer Key

MONEY

Problem	Answer		Problem	Answer
#1	1¢, 1 penny		#16	25¢, 1 quarter
#2	2¢, 2 pennies		#17	10¢, 2 nickels
#3	10¢, 1 dime		#18	20¢, 2 dimes
#4	3¢, 3 pennies		#19	16¢, 1 dime, 1 nickel, 1 penny
#5	5¢, 1 nickel		#20	20¢, 4 nickels
#6	5¢, 1 nickel		#21	26¢, 1 quarter, 1 penny
#7	5¢, 1 nickel		#22	50¢, 2 quarters
#8	2¢, 2 pennies		#23	6¢, 1 nickel, 1 penny
#9	15¢, 3 nickels		#24	7¢, 1 nickel, 2 pennies
#10	10¢, 1 dime		#25	31¢, 1 quarter, 1 nickel, 1 penny
#11	4¢, 4 pennies		#26	35¢, 2 dimes, 3 nickels
#12	40¢, 4 dimes		#27	50¢, 2 quarters
#13	5¢, 1 nickel		#28	18¢, 1 dime, 1 nickel, 3 pennies
#14	20¢, 2 dimes		#29	7¢, 1 nickel, 2 pennies
#15	1¢, 1 penny		#30	55¢, 2 quarters, 1 nickel

Coins

Coins

Money Pocket

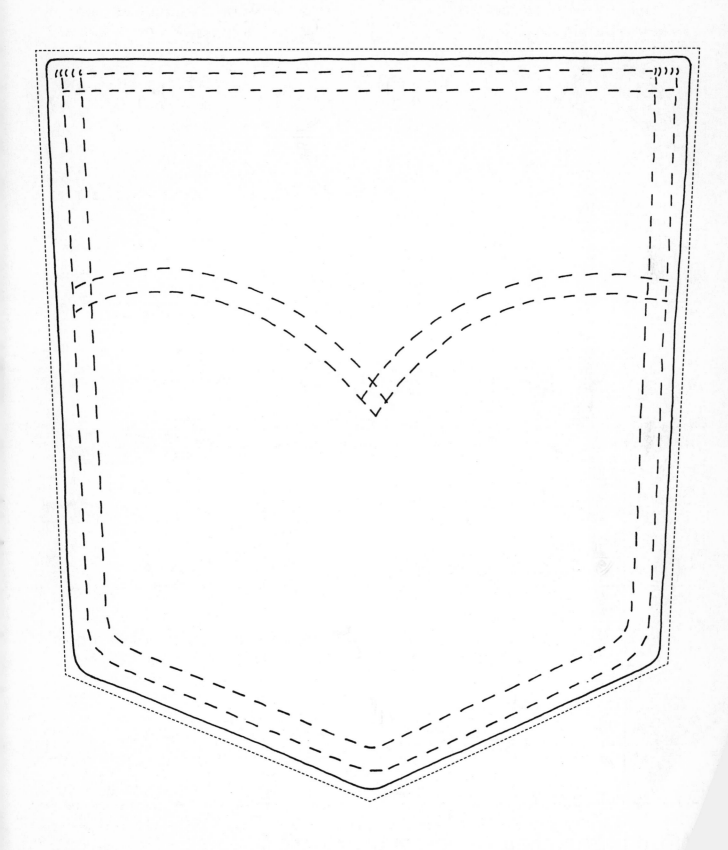

Name _____

1. Write a different time of day on the lines under each clock and draw the hands to match.

2. Write a word problem about one of the clocks. Use phrases such as <u>earlier than</u>, <u>later than</u>, and <u>exactly</u> to write your clues.

_____ : _____   _____ : _____   _____ : _____

_____

_____

What time does my clock show?

Name _____

1. Imagine you have a few coins in your pocket. Which coins would you choose? What would be the total value of those coins?

2. Write a word problem about the change in your pocket. Use words such as <u>more than</u>, <u>less than</u>, and <u>larger than</u> to write your clues.

_____

_____

the change in my pocket?